This Book Belongs to

TRAVEL IN SPACE
FLY
UFO
SPACE

Hello!

Welcome to
Outer Space

Good luck!

GALAXY
NEWS

Hunting the Star

meoww...

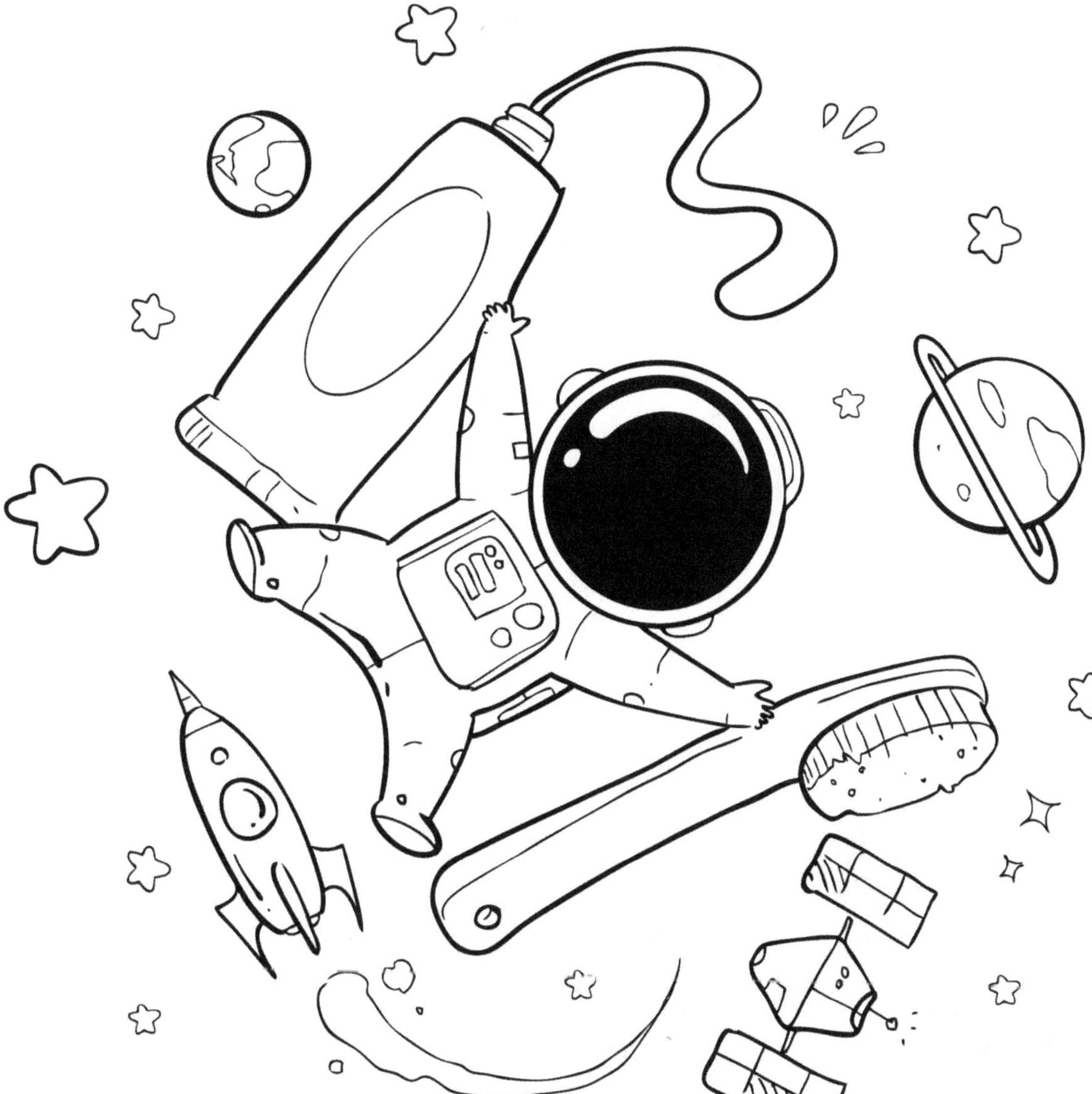

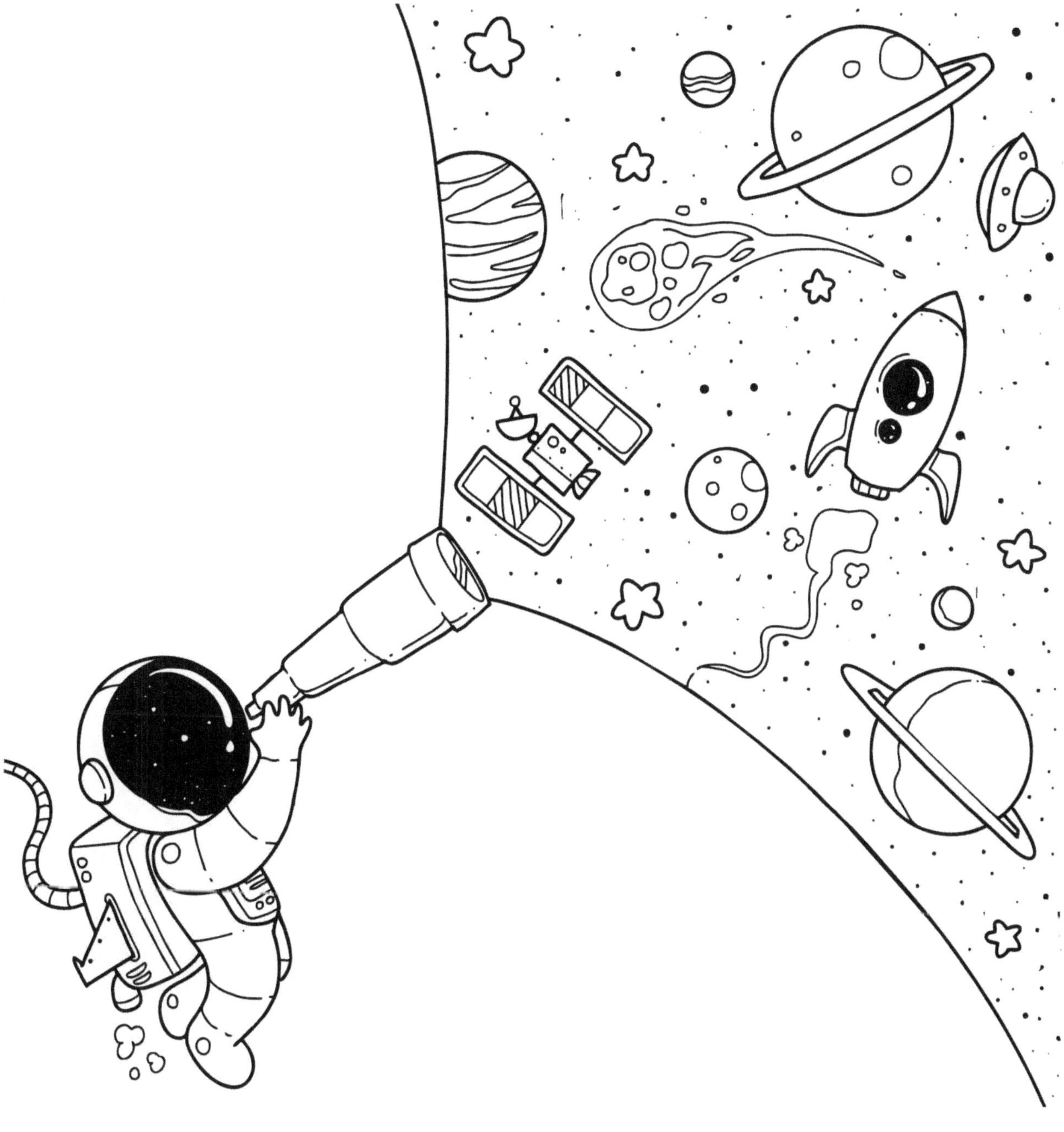

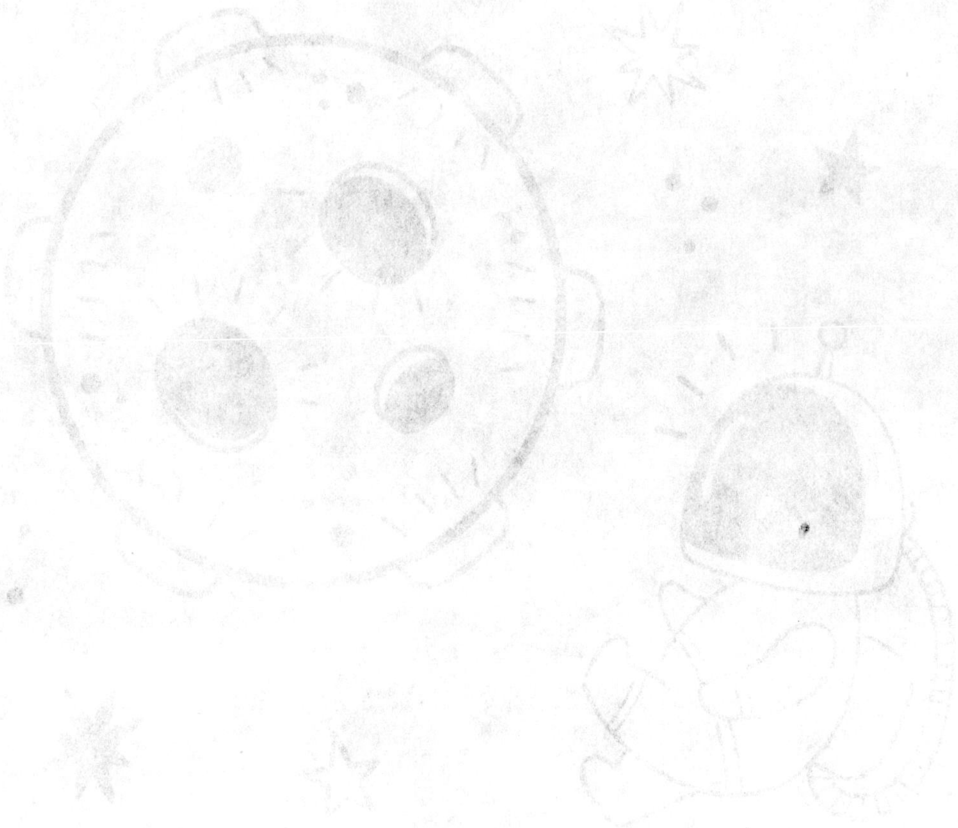

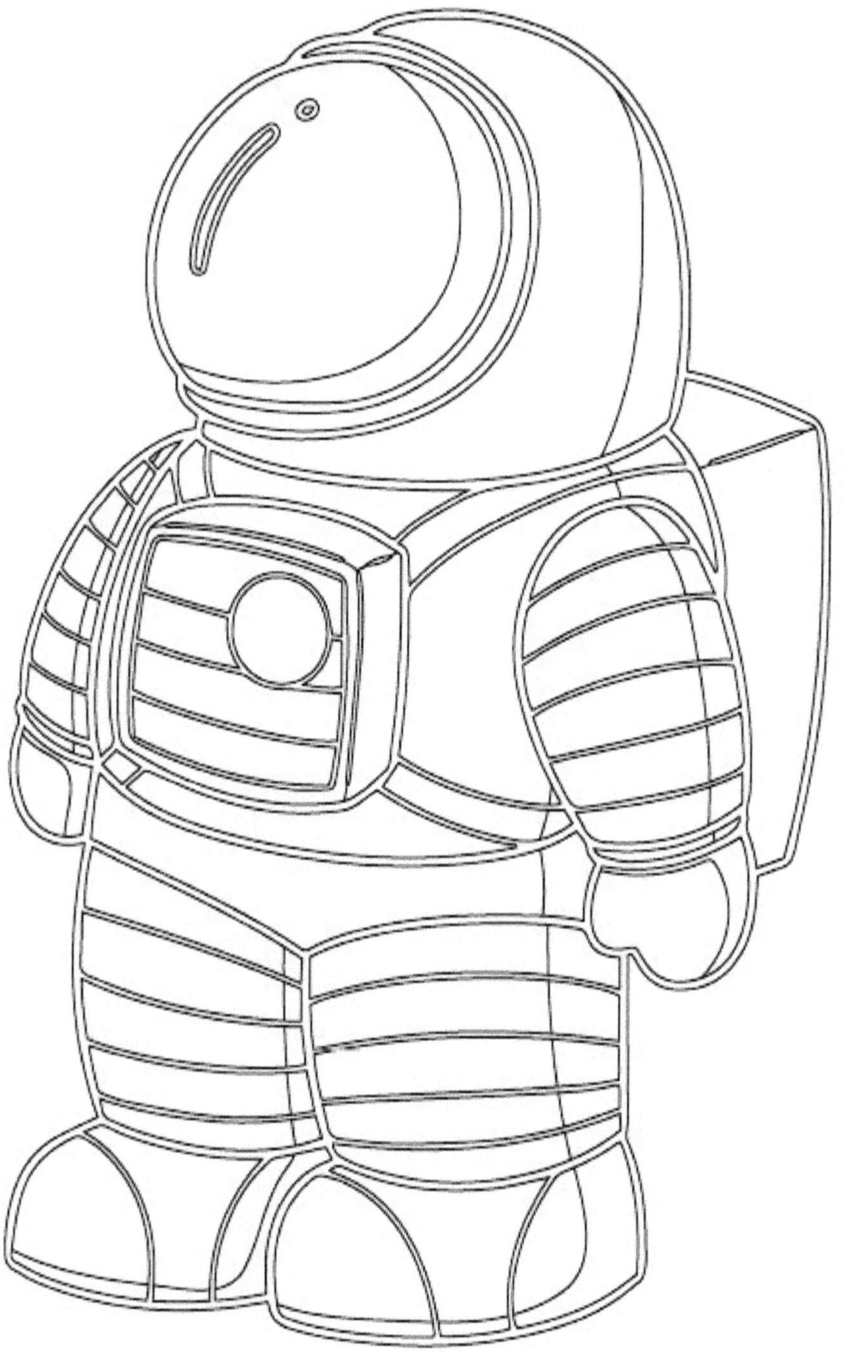

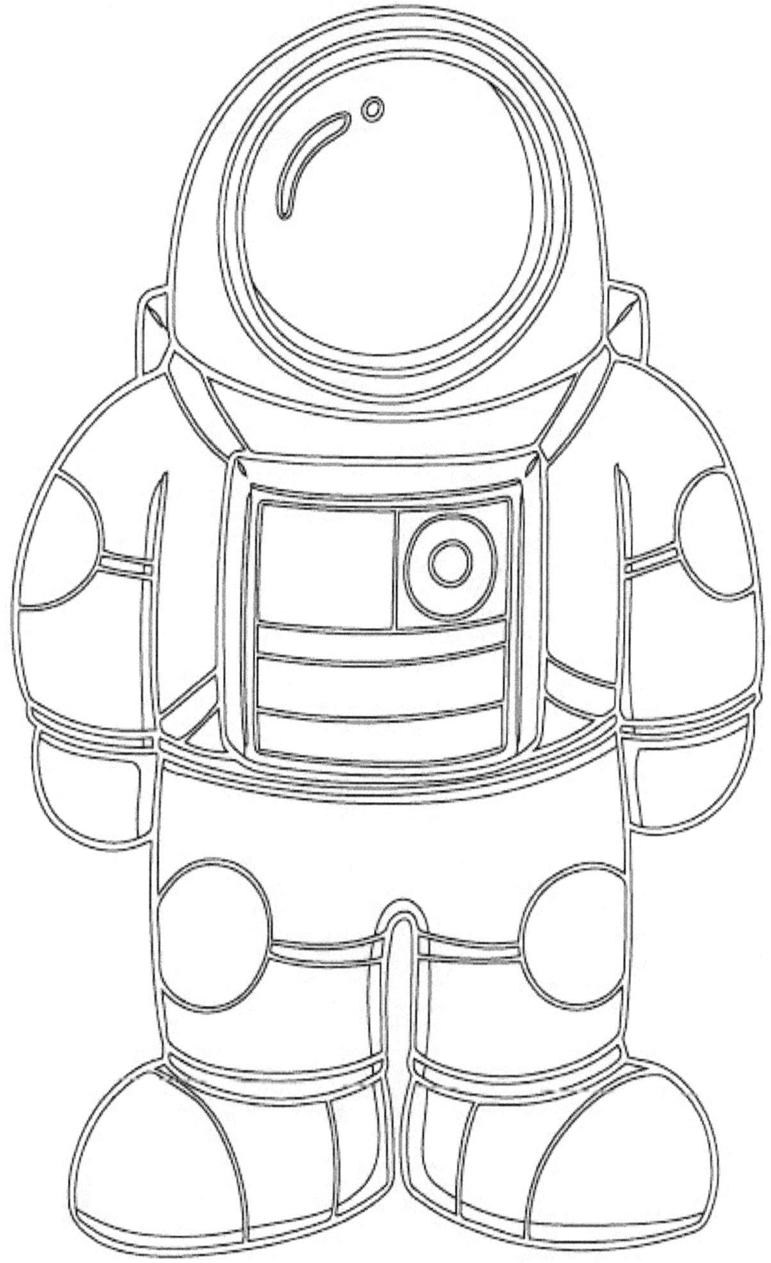

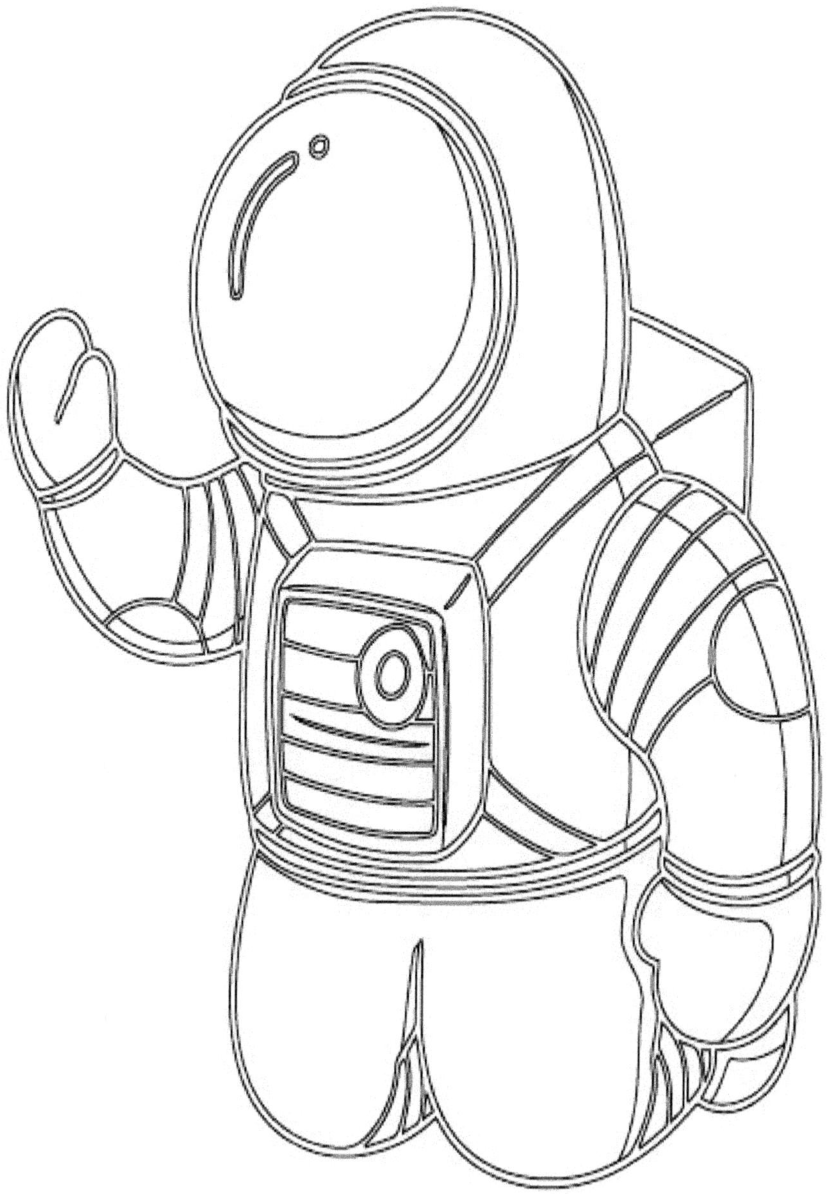

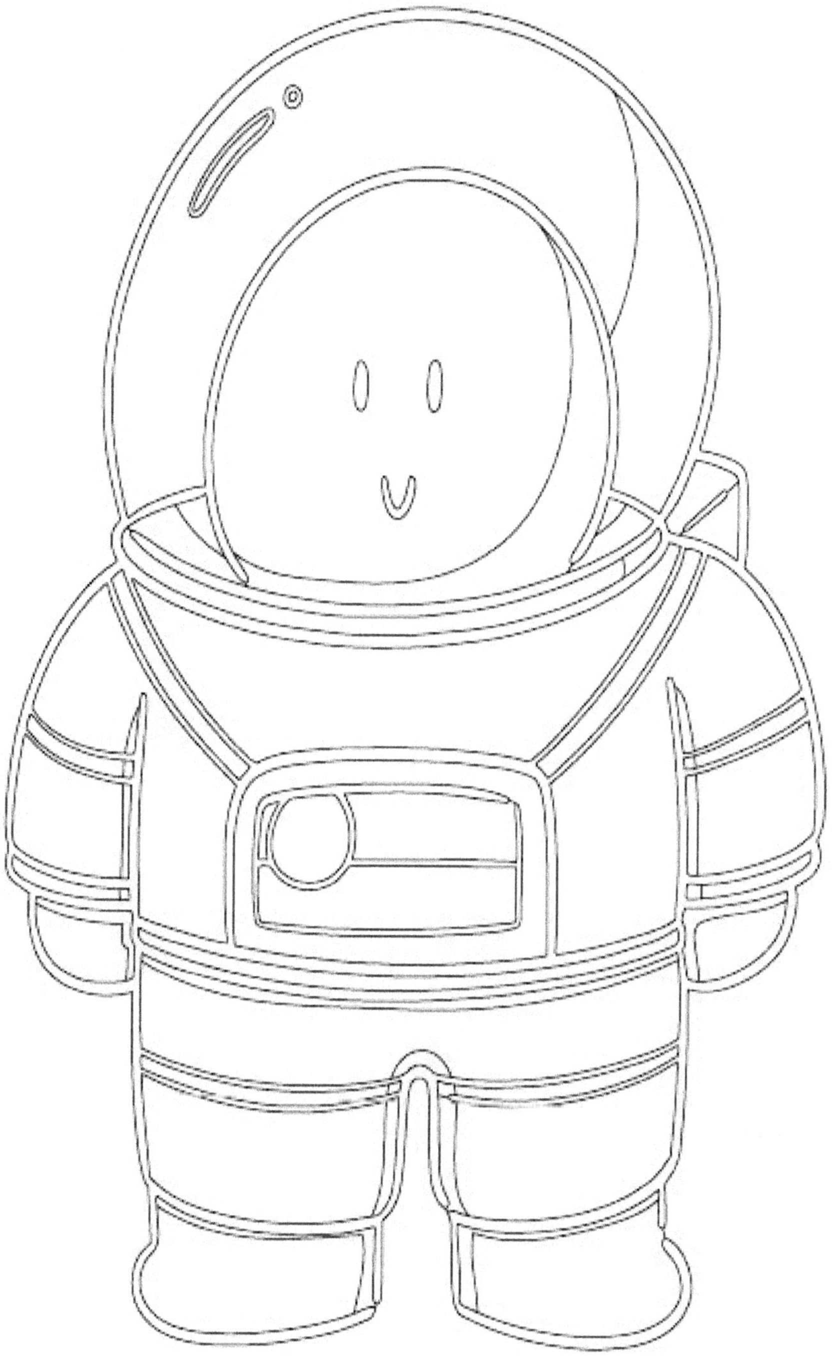

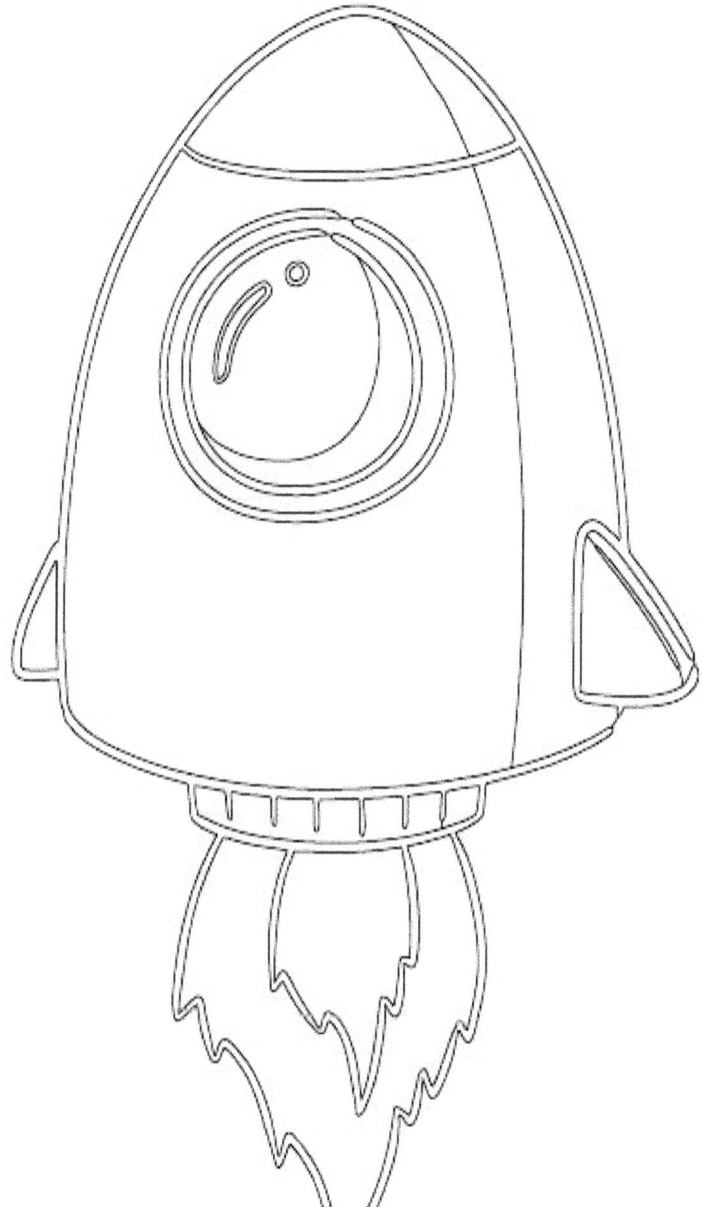

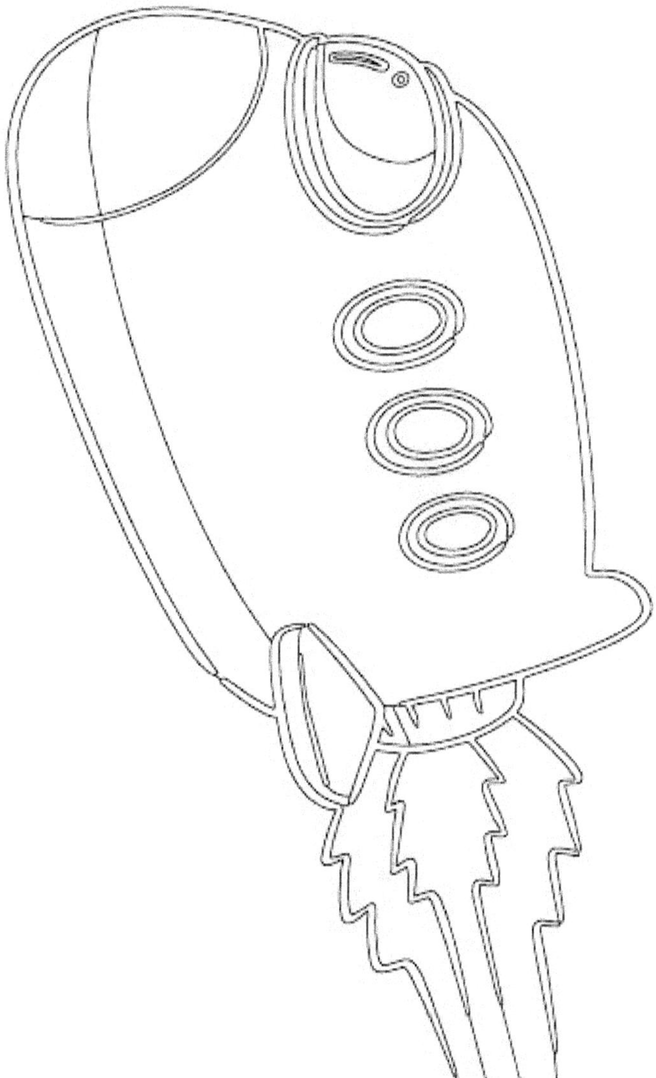

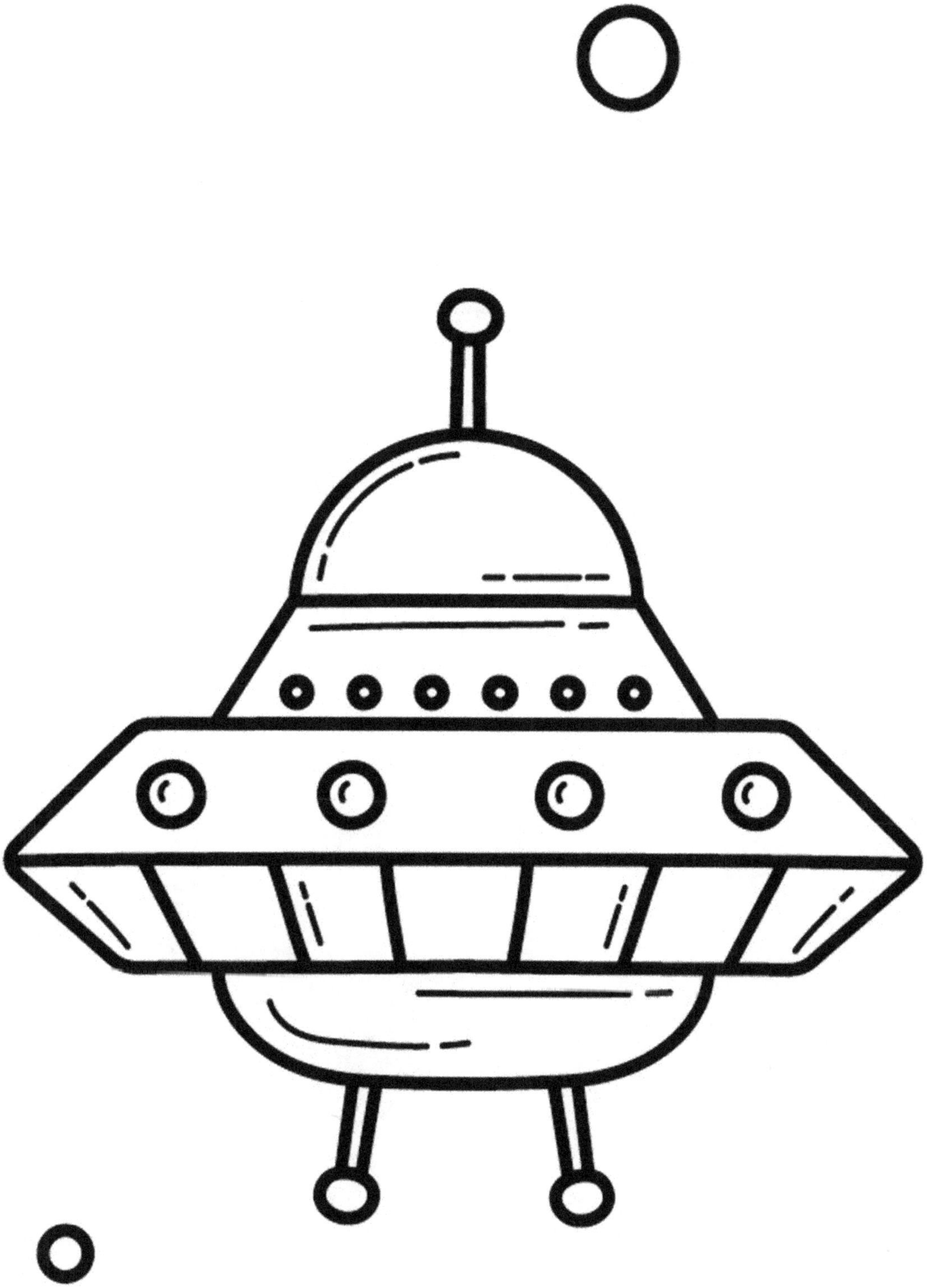

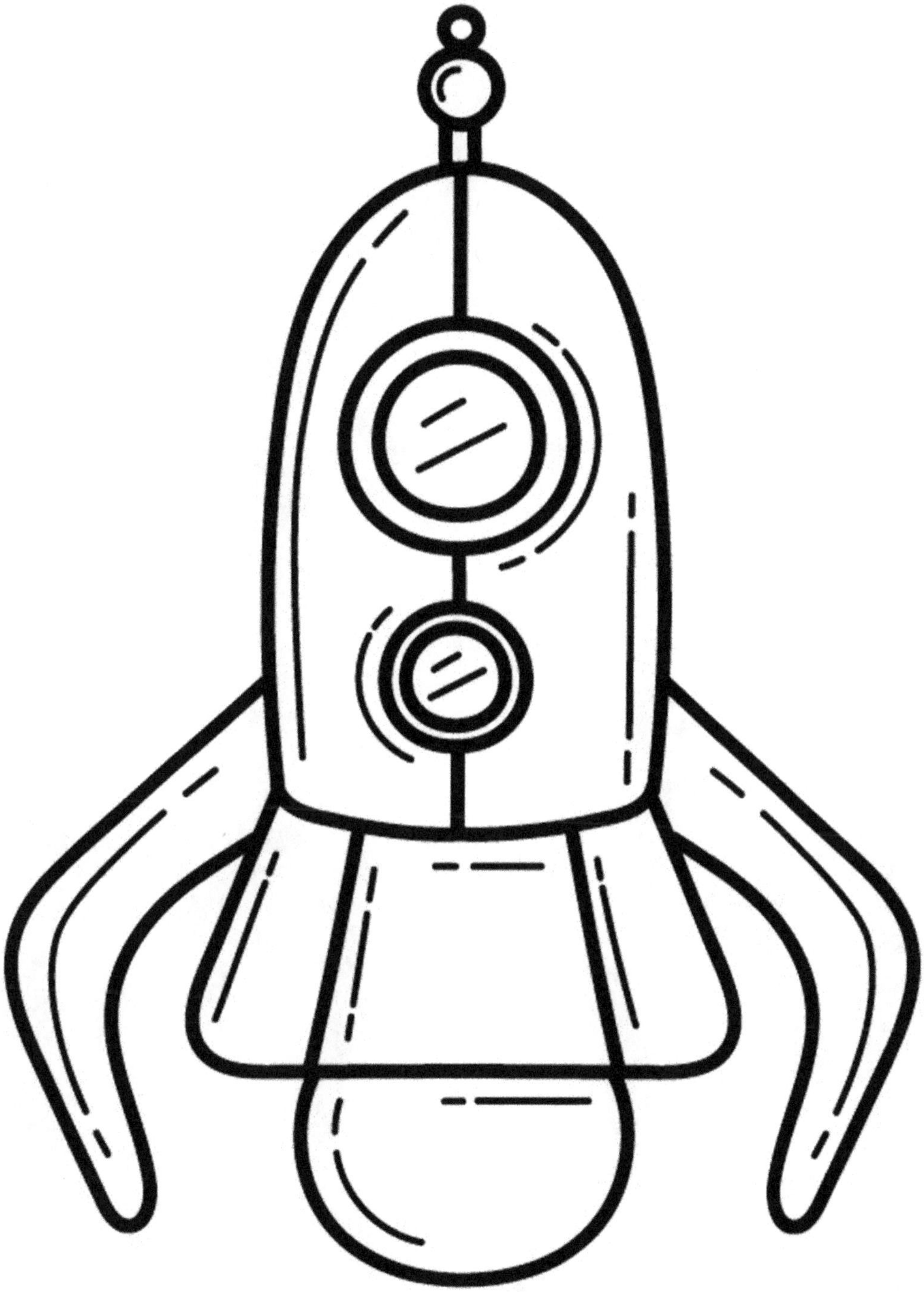

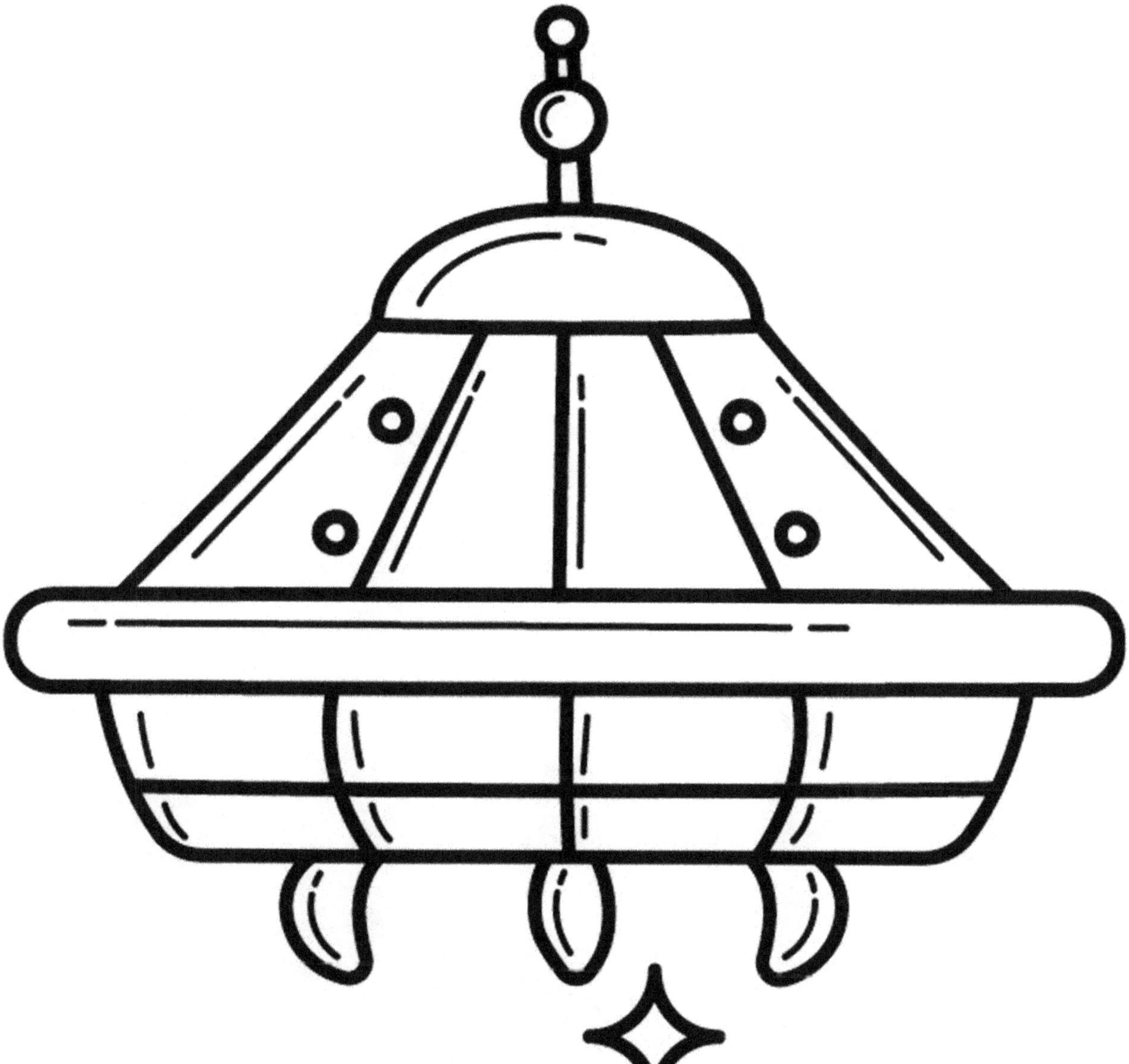

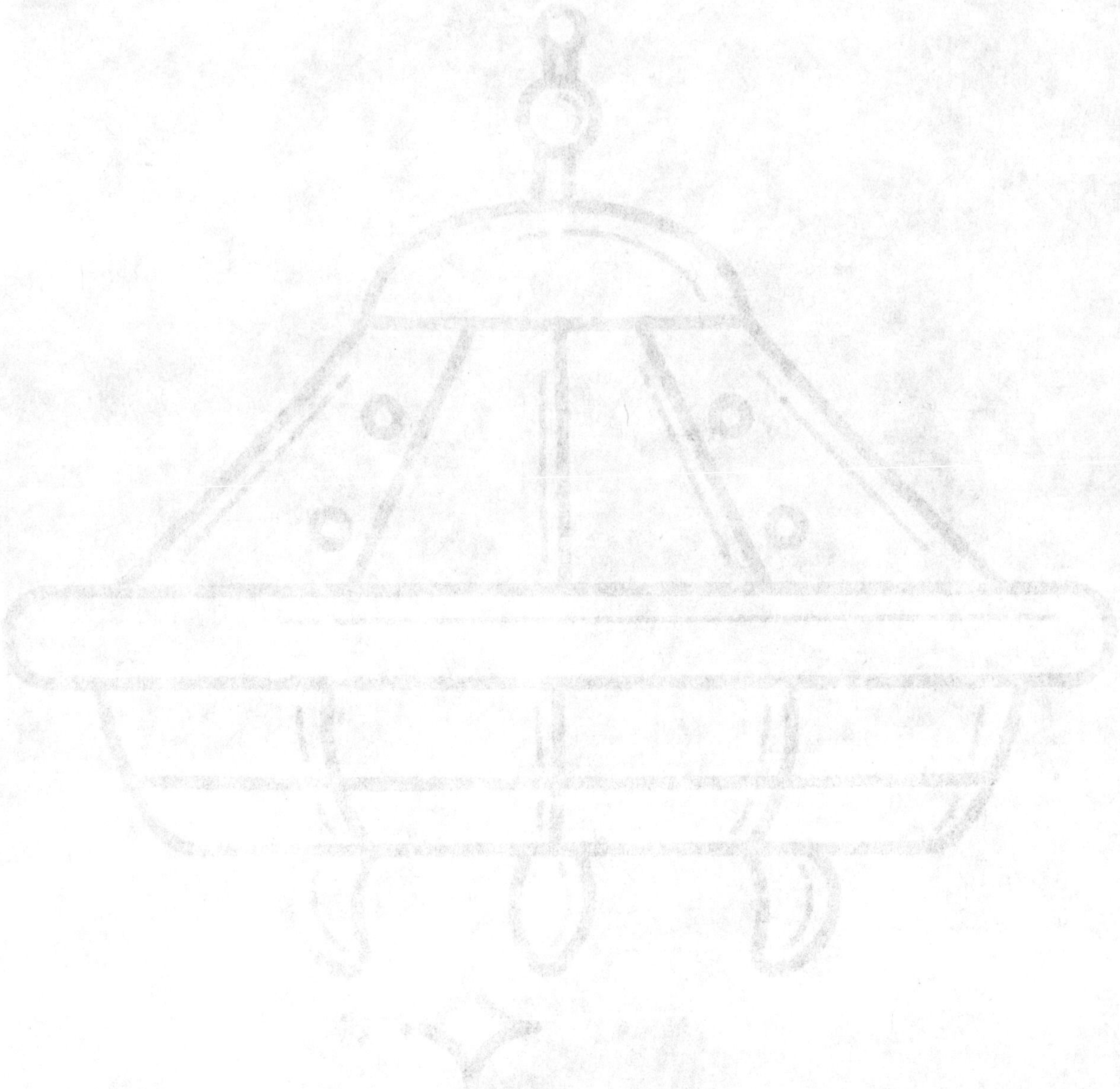

SPACE

SPACE ROCKET

Space

www.ingramcontent.com/pod-product-compliance
Lightning Source LLC
Chambersburg PA
CBHW080602060326
40689CB00021B/4914